Silence

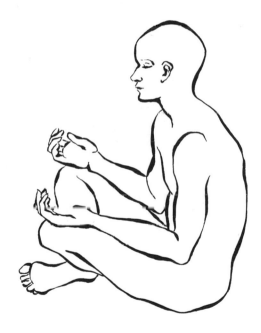

THE GIFTS

M. Jenelyn Wessler

# of SILENCE

Daniel B. Wessler

JOHN KNOX PRESS
ATLANTA

The Gifts of Silence is based upon four years
of experiencing by the authors leading
contemplative-celebrative weeks and weekends
with groups of all ages in many sections
of the United States.
You are welcome to use any portion of the text
or illustrations for your own or group silencing,
but no portion may be used for republication
without permission.

Royalties from the sale of this book will go
directly to the National Ghost Ranch Foundation.

Library of Congress Cataloging in Publication Data

Wessler, M   Jenelyn, 1924-
     The gifts of silence.

     1. Meditation. 2. Devotional exercises.
I. Wessler, Daniel B., 1924-   joint author.
II. Title.
BV4813.W48   131   75-32942
ISBN 0-8042-1613-4

acknowledgments

The many open, sharing, contemplative persons who have touched our lives with their gifts;

Marianthe and Ian, our daughter and son, for the hours spent posing for the *Gifts* drawings;

The Rev. James Hall and staff at Ghost Ranch, United Presbyterian education center in New Mexico, for inviting us to lead weeks of *Gifts* in peace among high mesas;

Selma Erlen, teacher of dance at the Jewish Community Center, Louisville, Kentucky, for increasing our awareness of how body and spirit respond as a whole;

To Jorge Enciso for inspiration from his book, *Design Motifs of Ancient Mexico;*

The following publishers:

From pp. 19 and 76 in *Hymn of the Universe* by Pierre Teilhard de Chardin. Copyright © 1965 by William Collins Sons & Co. Ltd., London and Harper & Row, Publishers, Inc. By permission of the publishers.

From *Resistance and Contemplation* by James W. Douglass, copyright © 1972 by James W. Douglass. Reprinted by permission of Doubleday & Company, Inc.

From p. 7 in *The Other Mexico* by Octavio Paz, copyright © 1972 Grove Press, Inc. By permission of the publishers.

From pp. 13, 91, and 92 in *On the Boundary* by Paul Tillich, copyright © 1966 Charles Scribner's Sons. By permission of the publishers.

From *The New English Bible.* © The Delegates of the Oxford University Press and The Syndics of the Cambridge University Press 1961, 1970. Reprinted by permission.

Daniel B. Wessler   M. Jenelyn Wessler

I am full, yet hungry.
How can I be fed?
Silence. Waiting night's
pregnant moment when earth
is empty, ready to be
filled with new day.
Silence, empty me of noise, worry, self-concern, mind's
ceaseless chatter. Ready me for your gift. Empty me.

Busy eyes see—grasp
what they want;
noisy ears hear—grasp sound.
World goes grey.
Silence. Empty, yielding, power
for sight and sound,
bright stars, bold noon.
Silence, replace my busy eyes and noisy ears with eye windows
and ear gates to receive your bright gift, awareness.

My life has been authored
by others. Where is my story?
Roots wither; branches dry.
Silence. Deep roots probing
reaches of dark earth,
branches exploring universe.
Silence, move me down mysterious depths where I have being.
Root me. Stretch me into heavens. Nourish my story.

I long to be touched deeply.
I need to be awakened,
gentled into sleep.
Silence. Caressing hands
mold being.
Silence, you know all my dimensions. Form me.

What is it in me
that pushes to be born?
The contractions startle me.
Silence. Powerful labor
of new birth,
pushing life.
Silence, womb me, push me.

What do—can I say yes to?
Silence. Burning, devouring,
healing, refining fire
reforms life.
I will celebrate affirmation of a new world,
new life, new person. Silence, refine me.

CONTENTS

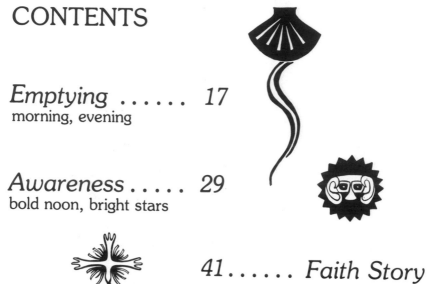

Emptying

Silence, empty me of noise, worry,
Self-concern, mind's ceaseless chatter.
Ready me for your gift. Empty me.

"There isn't a right way. You don't need to try so hard. Just sit there."

These are good words at the beginning of EMPTYING. They were spoken to a group who very much wanted to be successful in their silencing. Perhaps the group reflected the human desire to be approved, to do it right. Go ahead, do EMPTYING the way it works best for you. There isn't a right way.

We want you to begin by emptying yourself through body movement, then do breathing work, and then begin the mind clearing process. After we have worked through these we will reflect on what it means to empty yourself and create open, interior space.

Get down on the floor flat on your back on a hard surface. We will offer alternatives for those of you who for one reason or another are not floor liers at this time.

Okay, down on the floor, arms resting easily alongside your body. Point your right foot toward your head as tight as you can. Let your foot relax. Repeat. Point your left foot toward your head as tight as you can. Let it go. Repeat.

Lift your right leg a couple of inches off the floor. Stretch down hard. Let go the stretch and let your leg drop back into place. Lift your left leg off the floor. Stretch down hard. Let it drop. Repeat.

Make a fist with your right hand. Hard as you can make it. Let it go. Do it again. Make a hard fist with your left hand. Let it go. Do it again.

Raise the right arm just off the floor. Let it drop back. Do it again. Raise the left arm off the floor. Let it flop back. Repeat.

Raise both arms together toward the ceiling. Stretch up hard; reach that ceiling. Let the arms fall back easily at your sides. Repeat the movement.

Raise your shoulders up toward your ears as far as they will go. Let them drop back into place. Do it again. Again.

Clench your jaws, hard. Relax. Repeat, repeat.

Shut your eyes, hard. Relax. Repeat, repeat.

Scrunch up your whole face and wrinkle your brow. Hard. Relax, let it go. Do it again. Again.

How are you feeling now? Body alert, relaxed? Get a sense of that big toe down there. Feel it. Feel the floor pressing up against you.

Now run an inventory over your body from top to bottom checking for tension. Take your time. If your friend is reading these words to you, ask your friend to slow down and allow empty spaces between each movement. Savor your body feelings.

During the inventory did you spot tension points? If these points did not easily relax, don't try to relax them. Pay attention to the tension or soreness. What are these tensions saying to you? Our bodies are great communication systems and will tell us things we need to know. Once at this beginning point in a group a participant complained of a headache. She stayed with this ache until it told her about a phone call she had kept putting off. She left the group, made the call, her headache ceased, she went on with the silencing.

For those of you not down on the floor, go through these same exercises in a straight, hard chair. Point the toes up toward the head. Relax them. Raise your legs, make the fist, raise the arms. Do the rest of the movements. For an extra tension and release hang on to the seat or rungs of your chair with both hands and pull up as hard as you can. Release. Do it again.

Now will you stand.

Stand firm, feet well apart. Arms hang at the sides. Raise both arms up from your sides until your hands are directly overhead. Look up at your hands; let your head drop back. Stretch for the sky, the ceiling. Slowly lower your arms and look straight ahead. Do it again. Again.

Let your head drop forward as far as it will onto your chest. Relax the jaw; let your tongue rest easily in your mouth. Slowly rotate your head, first to the right, back, then to the left and forward. Repeat. Do it again if you wish.

Now bend forward in the waist, feet well apart, arms hanging down. You don't need to touch the floor; these are not calisthenics. Give some easy bounces up and down and then slowly unfold to an upright position being aware of each vertebra of your back as you unfold. Repeat. Repeat the movement again.

While you are standing upright, feet well planted on the floor, body open, circulation and energy flowing from feet to head, we want you to pay attention to your breathing.

Take a few deep breaths in through the nostrils, out through the mouth.

Where did you breathe? Some of us breathe with the shoulders, lifting them up a little with each breath. Some breathe with the collarbone and upper chest. We want you to locate your breathing deep down in the abdomen. If you are wearing a belt push against it on the intake of air. You may need to loosen it a few notches. Expand a tire right around your middle. No movement in shoulders or upper chest is necessary. In fact, you will produce tension and waste energy if you allow shoulder and upper chest movement. Breathe deeply, letting the diaphragm muscles push down into the lower abdomen to pull in the air. Now pay attention to how you exhale. Exhale through your slightly open mouth, tongue resting easily in your lower jaw. Exhaling takes no effort. Your rubber band muscles will push out the air as they involuntarily contract.

Inhale deeply. Now exhale very slowly. Very slowly.

Now we want you to begin a further concentration. As you slowly exhale begin counting. Think only of counting. Slowly: 1 2 3 4 5 6 7 8 9 . . . Let every bit of air be expended from your body. Empty it all out. You will probably find yourself counting up to about fifteen at first. Keep at it and in a few breaths you may be taking thirty seconds, or a count of 30 to empty out all the air. Don't try to set a record, but let all that breath be emptied out very slowly.

Now take a sitting position
on the floor or in a chair.
On the floor
sit tailor fashion,
legs folded and crossed,
torso upright,
head level
and looking
straight ahead.
Close your eyes.
　　Do your
deep breathing
and counting.

Make five inhalations and very slow exhalations keeping the count going. At the end of the fifth emptying do not breathe again until your body catches its breath. Experience the void at the end of the fifth emptying. That void is warm, peaceful, empty, open. It is the place of surprise and receiving.

Sometimes our minds just won't turn off as we do these preparations. Does your mind have a chatter all of its own when you shift into neutral? Go ahead, put it in neutral. Don't plan what you are going to think. Just listen to that mind of yours rattle away.

While you are listening to the mind wander wherever it wishes begin the deep breathing again. If the mind is really in the way, here is a help so you can get on with the silencing:

While you are breathing deeply, slowly, comfortably, we want you to take a fantasy trip. Imagine yourself on a grassy knoll in a meadow warmed by a yellow sun. There is a pathway leading from where you are sitting out across the meadow, over the rolling green

hills, far off into the distance where it disappears over the horizon. At your side is a little red wagon. In your fantasy wrap up your mind chatter into a package. Gift wrapped? Ribbons? Put the package into the red wagon. Slowly the wagon begins to move down the path away from you. You watch it as it moves across the rolling hills until it passes over the horizon and you are left quiet, warmed by the sun, relaxed.

You are sitting comfortably, relaxed, alert, breathing deeply and slowly, furthering the emptying process with every exhalation. Now you think of a bright shiny ball right in the center of your head. As you slowly exhale this ball begins to descend down through your body, falling very slowly with each exhalation, pausing with each inhalation. The ball passes through your body and begins its descent deep down into the heart of the earth. You have completed your first preparation for silencing, emptying, and opening your person.

There are distinct kinds of emptying. The first is that which produces absence and denies presence. To be empty in this way is to deny your own presence in the world, to deny the presence of your neighbor, and to deny the presence of God. This emptiness is a desensitized state in which you are present to or for no one. Numbness is another word for it. To respond to life with a prefabricated set of oughts is another description for it.

A second kind of emptiness is pre-planned emptiness of everything but the *good, true, and beautiful* in one's psyche. This avoidance of oneself leads to the half-person who floats apparition-like through life without touching or being touched either by suffering or rejoicing. This is selfishness in which one empties self only in order to receive self-selected gifts. It is an emptying with room for neither giving nor receiving. It is aggressive, self-concerned emptiness.

A third kind of emptiness prepares one to receive from the other person, prepares one to be surprised, truly gifted. Mary, the mother of Jesus, exemplifies this kind of emptying in her openness to the Annunciation: "Here am I," said Mary, "I am the Lord's servant; as you have spoken, so be it." (Luke 1:38 N.E.B.)

Jesus is described by Paul as having emptied himself of so-called heavenly prerogatives in order to make room for all kinds and conditions of persons: ". . . yet he did not think to snatch at equality with God, but made himself nothing, assuming the nature of a slave."

This positive emptying is the precondition for hearing and for speaking. If I am full of my own self and am caught in competitive, aggressive, success oriented idolatry I will listen to the other person all the while planning what to say next. This is aggressive listening that does not hear. It competes; it attacks. However, if I am empty before the other person there is space within me for my friend. There is risk in this creative emptiness. The other person may invade, seek to conquer, or, most risky of all, may respond to me with love and welcome me into his or her inner space.

Healing lies in the emptying process. Healing in family relationships, healing between colleagues, healing between friends have resulted from a shared emptying. There is also the possibility of physical healing of the body as a result of the emptying process. Relaxation of tension, improved breathing, opening of closed areas of the body for greater energy flow make for better health. Beyond this is the possibility that the integration resulting from emptying meditation may bring about the healing of sick bodies. There have been intimations of this in follow-up contacts with persons in groups with which we have worked.

The importance of deep breathing was brought home in one group by a counselor who spends much of her professional time working with depressed persons. She suggested to us that there is less oxygen in the blood of depressed people and that the stooped shoulders, carrying the load of depression, the sunken chest, and the collapsed abdomen initiate a vicious circle. Depression thrives on less oxygen and also creates that posture which in turn deprives the body of its full share of oxygen. The next time you are feeling depressed, check out your posture, breathe deeply, and see what happens to depressed feelings.

This is the miracle of Cross and Resurrection: God invites us into his inner space; he is empty before us. We know God in this way through Jesus in whom we see real power at work. His power is not self-fulfilling, arrogant. He does not crowd out others and fill inner space with self-will. His power gives, opens, empties, welcomes. This is the power great spirits have glimpsed as they seek a world peace based upon *welcome-in* love and not *keep-out* force.

Risks reside in the emptying process for which you have been preparing. You become vulnerable, open, startled, awe-struck by others, by self, by God.
It is risky, but it is creative,
energy filled,
exciting,
vital.

*thanks be to God
for this new day*

Awareness

Silence, replace my busy eyes and noisy ears
with eye windows and ear gates
to receive your bright gift,
awareness.

AWARENESS has to do with seeing and hearing that spring
from the depths of silent emptiness. It has to do with color, form,
music, and persons. The chapter concludes with a meditation on
the small and the large. The exercises are designed to intensify your
seeing and hearing.

But first, will you make your prepartion for AWARENESS

by going through the body movement and deep breathing you experienced in EMPTYING. Take your time. When you have completed your preparation, we will move on.

Let your eyes rove in exploration of what is around you. If you are indoors, explore the many colors of the room, its walls, furnishings. If you are outside, explore the colors of the sky, clouds, landscape close at hand and far off. If it is blue that attracts you, how many different shades of blue can you find? How many variations from dull to bright are there?

Now select one color. It may be the blue-green of a distant hill, a section of a painted wall, any color that draws you. As you intensify your emptiness through deep breathing, place the color in your mind at the center of a large blank circle. Now let your mind go into neutral and begin to fill that blank space with every association that your color brings forth. Stay with it. Let the color work in you to call up memories, scenes, persons, feelings and fill that space with these things. Don't be discouraged if this does not all happen in a flash. Let the leaven of color do its work. Take time.

This is a new way of seeing color. If we see color and simply name it *red, blue,* we have conquered color. However, if we see color with empty interior space ready to receive that color, we see it in terms of shade, intensity, feeling, association, memory. Color is a gift. Let your gift do its work in you.

    This time we want you to look around you and select a form to explore. The subject may be a tree, a rock, an art object in your room, a chair; it is your choice. Quietly explore the form of the subject. What are the shapes of its edges? How does it relate to other forms near it? What is the form of the space around your subject? What is the form of the empty space between your subject and a nearby form? Again, if we are full, form cannot feed us. We need empty spaces within to be explored by external forms.

    Return to your form. Begin to move away from it. How many empty spaces can you find around you? What are the shapes of these spaces? How are they bounded by the forms of subjects in relation to each other? The eye receives form into it to energize the body, mind. Stay with your meditation on the eye as a window to receive.

Now concentrate upon your hearing. You are quiet, alert, relaxed, continuing in your meditation. Put your ears into neutral and let in the sounds around you. Any sounds. Are there sounds that tell you the time of day? Are there sounds that tell you something about another person's work? Do some sounds make you feel at ease while other sounds make you tense? Can you hear people talking? What are they saying through their sound, not words, just sound? Are there happy, sad, anxious, loving, angry voices around you?

Now isolate one sound coming into your ears and place it in the center of a large blank circle. Put your mind into neutral and let the blank space be filled with all of the feelings and associations connected with that sound. Your ear-memory will keep it sounding, so it does not matter if the sound ceases during your meditation.

Music is a sound with gifts of its own. Select a favorite record or turn on your local radio station to music you want to listen to. If you have earphones put them on. Now sit or lie quietly, breathing deeply, silencing yourself, and let that music come in through your eargate. Put everything into neutral and let the music take you where it will. Are you flying, floating? What are you seeing? What are your feelings as the music moves you? Does your body want to move as the music plays you? Go ahead, move, play, enjoy, receive.

Here is another simple design for exploring listening awareness. Introduce your friend who is going to do this exercise with you to the preparation body movements and to the breathing so you will share a similar state of consciousness. Now sit opposite your friend and decide who will be speaker and who will be listener for the first round. When you have chosen your roles let the speaker talk to the silent listener for about three minutes. The listener will then repeat what the person has said in the listener's own words, bearing in mind the message given by the sound of the voice as well as the verbal content.

Speaker, did your listener accurately hear you? Did your listener pick up sound messages of which you were not aware? Did your listener's hearing reveal anything new to you about your message?

Now exchange roles and repeat the process of speaking, listening, and sharing the messages.

Once high above timberline we came across rock sheltered plants bearing flowers of exquisite, fragile beauty. Some among the climbers immediately called out the botanical name and passed on. Others stopped to open themselves to the flowers. Some had reached out to possess; others received vision as a gift. Immediate identification is like passing judgment. Openness and waiting are forms of love that enrich and vitalize life. As we ourselves are seen and heard by others in their deep silence and rich emptiness, we are known into being. Thus the process of becoming persons depends on our being in touch with seekers and listeners. Psalm 139 (N.E.B.) reveals the secret source of seeing and hearing:

Lord, thou hast examined me and knowest me.
Thou knowest all, whether I sit down or rise up;
    thou has discerned my thoughts from afar.
Thou hast traced my journey and my resting places,
    and art familiar with all my paths . . . .
Thou it was who didst fashion my inward parts;
thou didst knit me together in my mother's womb.
I will praise thee, for thou dost fill me with awe;
wonderful thou art, and wonderful thy works.
Thou knowest me through and through:
    my body is no mystery to thee,
how I was secretly kneaded into shape
    and patterned in the depths of the earth.

36   *Gifts of Silence*

*Select a small object and a large one within your field of vision. If you are outside, a flower, seed, or pebble will do for the **small**; a distant mountain or a great tree can be the **large**. If you are inside select a small art object, flower in a bouquet, any small item that particularly attracts your attention. For the large, is there something in view from your window that will do? Explore the **small** object fully; explore the **large** object. Let each in with your eye gate. When you have done this, center down on the meditation, **Small and Large**.*

Little flower, universe complete.
Wind, rain, snow, sun, rich earth, all seasons
work their wonder in you.
And they have formed me.
Our lives are rooted together.
A few days and you will seed.
Fall into the earth. Silence. New life.

Magic mountain, time etches you.
Wind, rain, snow, sun, have carved you.
You brook over the land; you collect time.
Mountain, you humble me, awe me, time me, silence me.

Your time, flower friend;
your time, mountain lord;
my time; all time;
God's time.
I am in God's time.
Birth time. Life time. Death time.
God's time.
One time.

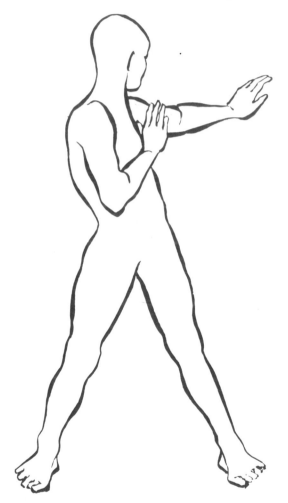

thanks be to God
for all the world around me

for all I will experience

Faith Story

Silence, move me down mysterious depths
Where I have being. Root me.
Stretch me into heavens.
Nourish my story.

In this chapter we want you to explore your deeper roots, your higher branches. We want you to become aware of your faith story.

Begin as usual with the body relaxing movements on the floor or sitting in a chair. Add a new dimension to the exercises you do standing:

You are standing erect, your feet well apart and planted firmly on the floor or the earth. Think of your roots extending from your feet down into the earth. You are rooted in the earth, in the place of nourishment. Rains wash nutrients into the earth; your roots are secretly fed by deep springs. Close your eyes. Let your roots move down into deep earth. Tap root. Tendrils.

Now lift your arms, head falling back, eyes looking at your hands overhead. Stretch those arms into the sky. You are reaching your branches. Follow that stretch to where it takes you. Let it stretch. Your branches are in the heavens. Clouds move among your branches. Moist clouds bring life. The sun bathes you with its warmth. You stretch upward as far as your reach will take you, and you root downward into the mysterious places of your nourishment.

As you do your deep breathing let your roots move more deeply into the earth with each exhalation. Breathe in, full, deeply into the abdomen. Breathe out slowly and as you empty yourself let your roots move downward. Do not try to add content to your roots. That will come. Let those roots form in your fantasy. Let them probe deeply. As you breathe let your branches feel the sun, rain, wind of the sky. Probe. Stretch.

Roots probe deeply into rich earth.
Where are my places of feeding?
Roots touch springs.
Where are my places of refreshment?
Roots move into earth's foundation.
Where is my security?
Branches reach sunward.
Where is my light?
Branches open.
To whom do I pray?
Thank God for roots and branches.

A faith story is the account of the development of a person's faith through dry time, rich time, fearful time, trusting time, young time and old time. Sometimes it is the story of relationships with people who have been seminal in our lives. Sometimes it is the story of struggle and wrestling. The story may have many colors. Sometimes it is an account with an unbroken line running through it; at other times it is a disconnected series of heights and depths. A help to some in developing their faith story has been to recall how they have reacted to the word G O D from earliest memory to the present moment, both in saying yes and saying no.

Tell your faith story first of all to yourself. Take a large sheet of paper, the larger the better. On it draw your faith story with crayons or paints. Some of you may make it a symbolic account that would be a mystery to a stranger looking at it. Some may make your drawings very representational. It doesn't matter. This is not necessarily a work of art, but it is to inform you. Take your time, but try not to think too much before you draw. Let the colors and the movement of your hands as you draw lead you into your faith story. However you express yourself, remember it is yourself. No critic is going to judge your work; no theologian will grade your language. It is your story. Claim it. Take all the time you need to develop your drawing.

When you have finished, share your drawing with someone whom you trust, who perhaps has a faith story drawing to share with you. You may want to record your story on tape. If you do this, then you have both yourself to listen to and the drawing to look at as you become more aware of your faith roots in the past, present, and even into future projection.

Roots and branches eventually lead to a person's story. This faith story may be couched in religious language or it may contain no so-called religious words. The story may not name God, but it will lead into places and persons of nourishment, as well as places and persons of hunger. Thirst and satisfaction are in the story. Each story is different. Not only are stories individually different, but persons at different ages and at different stages in their lives tell different stories. Does the story really change? Was the story told at one stage more true than the other?

Think of how the story of a family by one of its members changes. Do you tell the same story of your family as you did when you were a teenager, a young seeker, in middle age? The facts remain the same. New meanings are added and half-forgotten incidents and relationships suddenly appear highlighted.

But what if you had no story? You would suffer from amnesia. When asked, "Who are you, friend?" you could give data about yourself, where you live, social security number. Without a story you would be a collection of unrelated data. Thank God for everyone who can tell his or her story.

It has been our experience in leading groups in the *Gifts of Silence* that everyone has a story. Sometimes it takes a long time with aching and rejoicing, laughter and tears, surprises, before that story comes into consciousness, but there is always a story.

When the Christian community gathers for worship it is a story time, a time of remembering. How many of us claim Abraham as part of our story? The Judeo-Christian faith can graft us into a story that transcends our own short stories. This is true not only for Christianity and Judaism. Many so-called primitive people gather in communal ceremony to hear their story and to be thus grafted into the tribe. In many initiation and passage rites the secrets of the origins of the tribe are shared so that the new member will have his or her complete story. How sterile worship or ceremony would be if it confined the people's story to a span of one or two generations.

Story is essential in the development of a child to an adult who has a sense of identity. It is equally vital in the development of a people or nation. Power is in the hand of that political leader who can restore a nation's lost identity. This can be a demonic power when a Hitler is able to re-identify a people with a new story, or when a slave owner imposes a new name on a field worker, or when a conqueror de-stories the myths and religion of a people, or when a man imposes an identity story upon a woman.

This identity producing faculty of the story opens the door to potency. The potent story teller is able to identify critical authors from his or her story's past; is able to make a choice between the persons and forces who bid for authorship in the present. The potent story teller is able to be thankful for past authors who have valued his or her story and does not have to claim or boast sole authorship.

In our relationships with other people we can never be certain when we are co-authoring their stories. Parents can never be aware totally of their authorship in their children's lives. At this time, in whose life are you playing an authorship role? Authors we will be. The question is what meanings, symbols, hopes, fears are we contributing to another's story. One of the wonders of being human is the value we can have for each other as co-authors. What a day in the life of our world it will be when nations cease de-storying each other, when peoples value each other's stories and become potent co-authors in the common human story of nurtured roots and reaching branches.

thanks be to God
for the sky overhead
the sun and the rain

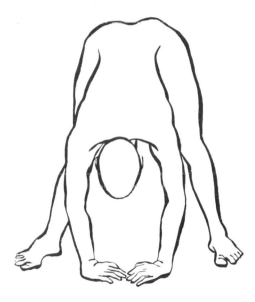

for the earth beneath my feet

Trust

Silence,

you know all my dimensions.

Form me.

When you have completed your body stretching and relaxing movements, sit down in your deep breathing position. Place your hands at ease, palms upward in a comfortable position resting on your knees. Begin your meditation upon trust by looking at your hands with an appreciation for all they do for you. It is a long list, so take your time. They open a door, put food in your mouth, comb your hair, and on and on.

As you rest your hands easily upon your knees, palms upward, consider the hand language we use. "I give you my hand on it." A little old-fashioned, but still in use: "He took her hand in marriage." Both of these are trust signs. When we swear an oath it is with the hand raised, palm outward. In anger we give "the back of the hand." We make an offering with the palm upward; we bless with the palm downward upon the blessed person. We close the hand to make a fist in violence, protecting the palm, the hand's soft underbelly.

An exercise with clay has helped many people get a close sense of the hand. If you have a clay deposit in a near field use this natural clay with a little water, sand, and some ashes mixed in. The mixing with the hands is part of the enjoyment and a good beginning in letting hands do their thing. If no clay deposit is at hand you can usually find clay at a school supply store or at a ceramic supply shop. But be sure to buy real clay, not plasticine.

Take another look at your hands before you begin to work your clay. Appreciate your hands. Then let them begin to work your clay. Trust the clay; don't force your will upon it. Trust your hands; don't pre-plan how they are going to work the clay. When you have completed a form sit before it and ask the clay and your hands what they have told you. You might cover your form with a damp cloth and a piece of plastic so you can return to it later to let it speak again.

This is uncompetitive play. Can you trust yourself just to play?

As you sit contemplating your hands once more, think of them as your trust agents that extend and receive trust through touch. It is your open, empty hand that touches, that extends trust. Let your deep breathing move you into meditation upon your own emptying, uncovering, disarming in order to receive and to extend the trust touch.

In the absence of trust, emptying is greatly inhibited, sometimes impossible. If you are experiencing some difficulty with your emptying and silencing check out the trust level at which you generally operate most of the time. This trust level can be measured in part by the way you feel when you first enter a room of strangers. Do you expect them to welcome you? Or do you expect them to turn a cold shoulder? How do you react to new situations, changes in plans? Where there is a generally high interior trust level, "I trust life," emptying is much easier. Where there is fear or feelings of unworth, emptying is more difficult. Fear and feelings of unworthiness are often expressed through a denial of the body. This really gets in the way of emptying and meditation which rely so much on the body. Denial of the body is another way of saying, "I cannot be affirmed as a worthy, valued instrument." It is another way of saying, "I do not trust God's creation." It is one more way of saying, "I don't trust me."

There are clear signs of fear and mistrust that we easily recognize in ourselves and each other. For example, when we habitually tell others how very busy we are, we make it clear that there is little empty space inside us for their presence. When we must always be busy doing something or being entertained by TV or games or such, we give clear signals of the lack of interior space. When we are over-serious and have trouble with relaxed, purposeless playing we give a clear indication of lack of trust and the ability to be empty. Perhaps a witness to our faith is the ability to be playful in our religious life.

Another signal to ourselves of riches or poverty in our trust is our need to be in control. Probably you can recall from your own experience situations in which trust has been negated by the need to be in control. When the control factor is high others will know you are flying a warning signal, "I don't trust you." Or is it, "I don't trust myself."

Most of us trust.
We run trust risks.
Sometimes these risks
turn out badly
when trust is
misused,
betrayed, or
rejected.
How do we react
to the situation
of broken trust?
We are tempted
to cease trusting
if we have been
burned in a
trust relationship.
We are tempted
to build up the armor,
close the hand,
fill the empty space,
get out of touch.

We so easily use the word, *reconciliation*. Confrontation of the real issue in broken trust can be replaced by cheap forgiveness, an off-hand, "Oh, it's okay." If confrontation at the trust level is undertaken and it works out, then the broken relationship will be restored. It will not be restored to its former nature; the broken trust will always be a part of the *story* of the relationship. But a new trust level between the persons will be achieved. If the confrontation does not work out and either party runs away or fights, then reconciliation will not have taken place. This is risk; reconciliation does not always work out. A breakdown in trust may lead to the death of the relationship.

What of prayer and trust?

The conventional prayer posture is with hands together at chest level, arms against the body, head bowed, eyes closed. Take this posture yourself. What areas of the body are exposed? What areas are protected? Soft underbelly is well protected by the arms, palms of the hands are protecting each other, hard skull plate is all of the head that is visible.

Now take the position that was originally a prayer posture for the early Christian community. Body is standing, erect; head is tilted slightly up, eyes are open and the arms are raised, palms towards the heavens. What are the open elements in this posture?

In the language of prayer we can reveal posture towards God. One prayer is silent, open, emptied, expectant. Another prayer is a wordy asking from already filled interior space. One prayer is a pouring out; another prayer is a parade of plans for God's action. One prayer is full of awe; another prayer defines and limits the spirit.

A gift of silence is emptiness, trust, before God.

No words.

Trust.

Silence.

Interior space—expectant.

I will stretch into change

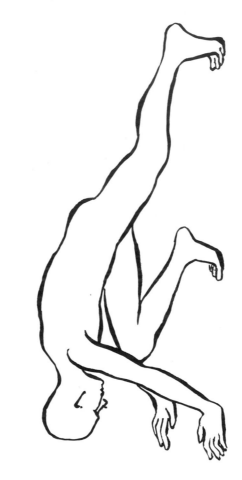

I will stretch into new relationships

Rebirth

Silence, womb me.
Push me.

Many new beginnings, re-births, pilgrimages are begun while fasting. It is not surprising that after having been greatly valued in the past, today the fast is being rediscovered by many as a cleansing, renewing discipline. Sometimes people think of the fast as something that happens only within the seclusion of the cloistered community. As with most stereotypes this is not the whole story. The fast in seclusion is a rich experience, but it can occur just as well in the school, in business, in secret by individuals who are going about their daily routines, during social reform action, or by groups on retreat.

"During the fast I felt I was being molded." "Once the hunger pains were gone I experienced new insights about myself and my world." "Prayer changed for me during the fast. I was more aware of God's presence and did less asking." "During the fast we decided not to keep working on our marriage." "After the second day everything seemed much clearer and brighter to me. I felt more alive than every before." "My head ached. I felt sick. I'll never try that again." "Sounds were brighter. My music took on new dimensions." "I am going to change political parties as the result of insights gained during the fast." "It was very disappointing. Nothing happened." "I don't think it was good for my health." "I couldn't stand to be near food while I was fasting. The refrigerator and I had a fight. I won! I'm going to lose weight now. I know why I'm overweight and I don't need that anymore." "Yes, I felt very empty. Spiritually empty. Vacant. Then insights, ideas, commitments began forming in me. They seemed to come of themselves. I was not pushing."

These are paraphrases of comments made by people in their evaluations of the fast experience as a part of a week or weekend of the *Gifts of Silence*. The location of group experiences in fasting has been college campuses, theological seminaries, the wilderness, and retreat centers.

At the week long *Gifts of Silence* on Ghost Ranch, the United Presbyterian Church education center in New Mexico, the setting for fasting is Long House, a Navajo type gathering place open to light and air, with a dirt floor and beamed roof overhead.

Near at hand are the teepees where the thirty members of the *Gifts of Silence* group dwell. There are adults and young people, men and women, and ages vary from thirteen to seventy.

The day we celebrate rebirth is almost with us. This is our preparation:

"The group will meet this evening to initiate the fast. In response to questions from some of you about the experience, here are some simple directions for your own welfare during the period of fasting. First, drink plenty of water. We are in a high, dry country and dehydration won't help anyone who is fasting. Plenty of water means a couple of glasses every two or three hours. Do not let this water intake control you, but on the other hand, do stop for a drink when you pass the fountain or go to the bathroom. No, we won't be taking any solids or fruit juice. Take some extra rest. A *siesta* in the afternoon is a good plan at this high altitude. You may experience some discomfort during the first hours, but again you may not. This varies from person to person. If you are uncomfortable, don't pop an aspirin. Do the relaxing exercises, deep breathing, and in your meditation move right through that discomfort. What if it doesn't go away? It won't hurt you. If anyone is under a special medication or on a prescribed diet, why don't you go ahead and follow your medical instructions, but keep with the group through all the disciplines of the fast except the no food part? Greet others on the Ranch who are not part of our group just as you would if you were not fasting. Between us, however, let's speak to each other only with mutual consent. At other times, remain silent and do not interrupt each other's meditation.

"In your preparation for our Initiation of the Fast tonight, get a clear insight into why you are fasting. Some of you may want to fast with world peace in mind. Others may want to fast mindful of a person who is in special need. You will want to enter the fast with emptiness. If we discover this evening that there is a consensus and we want to fast with a group purpose, we will do that. If any of you make a redecision about this and do not plan to fast, let the group know tonight, but do plan on keeping with all the disciplines except the not eating."

That night the group met with a variety of reasons for fasting that spanned the spectrum from world peace to an openness to healing, to just plain curiosity. Two passages of scripture were circulated, one to the men, one to the women, with the request that during the fast each person spend some hours with the passage.

The men were given a passage from the Gospel according to Luke:

> So he came to Nazareth, where he had been brought up, and went to synagogue on the Sabbath day as he regularly did. He stood up to read the lesson and was handed the scroll of the prophet Isaiah. He opened the scroll and found the passage which says,
>> "The Spirit of the Lord is upon me because he has anointed me;
>> he has sent me to announce good news to the poor,
>> to proclaim release for prisoners and recovery of sight for the blind;
>> to let the broken victims go free,
>> to proclaim the year of the Lord's favour."
> He rolled up the scroll, gave it back to the attendant, and sat down; and all eyes in the synagogue were fixed on him.
> He began to speak: "Today," he said, "in your very hearing this text has come true." (Luke 4:16-21 N.E.B.)

The women were given this passage from the Gospel according to Luke:

> And Mary said:
> "Tell out, my soul, the greatness of the Lord,
> rejoice, rejoice, my spirit, in God my saviour;
> so tenderly has he looked upon his servant,
>> humble as she is.

For, from this day forth,
all generations will count me blessed,
so wonderfully has he dealt with me,
    the Lord, the Mighty One.
    His name is Holy;
his mercy sure from generation to generation
    toward those who fear him;
the deeds his own right arm has done
    disclose his might:
the arrogant of heart and mind he has put to rout,
    but the humble have been lifted high.
The hungry he has satisfied with good things,
    the rich sent empty away.
He has ranged himself at the side of Israel his servant;
    firm in his promise to our forefathers,
he has not forgotten to show mercy to Abraham
    and his children's children, for ever." (Luke 1:46-55 N.E.B.)

    Early one morning during the fast at Ghost Ranch we arose in darkness to make our ascent to Chimney Rock before sunrise. We were pilgrims winding up the high mesa to the promontory before which the land spread in a great basin ringed round with mountains. In silence we climbed; in deeper silence we waited for the dawn. As the sun began to rise from the eastern horizon, blood red color spilled down the western mountains. Awe settled into our spirits. We were reading aloud from Teilhard de Chardin:

    Over there, on the horizon, the sun has just touched with light the outermost fringe of the eastern sky. Once again, beneath this moving sheet of fire, the living surface of the earth wakes and trembles, and once again begins its fearful travail. I will place on my paten, O God, the harvest to be won by this renewal of labour. Into my chalice I shall pour all the sap which is to be pressed out this day from the earth's fruits.

My paten and my chalice are the depths of a soul laid widely open to all the forces which in a moment will rise up from every corner of the earth and converge upon the Spirit. Grant me the remembrance and the mystic presence of all those whom the light is now awakening to the new day.

The reading ceased. The sun poured its light. Flights of swallows whirred up the cliff face, soaring to meet new day. We made our descent, silence holding the sunrise moment and the words of Teilhard de Chardin in interior space. With emptiness we moved into our individual spaces to let the scriptures do their work in us. We were being molded by the good hands of God.

Other dawns have done their work in us. There have been uncanny first lights in a silent city, smoky sun over chimney pots in a Scottish burgh, shimmering sunrise on a Kenya plain, mysterious sculpturing by dawn light of the interior valley of Mexico below Popocatapetl's snowy peak, first light through branches of ancient pines of a Japanese garden. Perhaps it was the intense and powerful silence of that group, perhaps it was a special gift of emptiness ready to receive, perhaps the Spirit was moving, but of all the silent dawnings, it is the dawn on Chimney Rock that remains sharpest, most fresh, and most easily recaptured.

New beginnings are like interior dawnings. They are as varied as persons are different. New beginnings are always possible. We want you to locate some new beginning you would like to launch. When you have completed your body movements and are settled into your meditation, run through an inventory of your relationship with specific people. Run through an inventory of your work areas, that is, boundaries of your life where you feel you are on important breakthrough edges. Center down on one in particular. Place this work area or relationship in the center of a large blank circle in your mind. Let everything that comes to mind form in the circle. Take plenty of time. Don't be afraid. When something very good comes into the picture, stay with it. It is a way of being thankful. When you are tempted to close the door on some area leave the door open and let whatever will form in the circle. The discomfort of letting in what you would prefer to avoid may be the most productive of your efforts in this exercise.

Now center down in one area of the picture on something

you would like to change, *not in another person,* in yourself. Stake a claim to this new beginning. Take all the time you need.

When you have worked out the new beginning you wish to make for yourself, write it down. Make a contract with yourself. Make it specific and manageable. Deal with specifics, not generalities such as, "I will be more creative," "I will be more forgiving," "I will take more initiative." When you have it written down, put it where you can easily check back every now and then to see how you are doing. In a few days you may wish to do this exercise again and renegotiate your contract, adding new dimensions, changing others. If you are reading this with a friend or your spouse, place your friendship or marriage in the circle and do the same thing as above, then compare your new beginnings contracts and check them out with each other.

When you contract with yourself for new beginnings you enter into a pilgrimage. Usually religious pilgrims are on their way to a shrine with a specific destination and route in mind. Not so the pilgrim of the spirit who makes new beginnings. We travel not with certainty but with trust. Persons who travel like this need to travel light. Here is your question: In order to make a new beginning, in order to start a pilgrimage, in order to pull up stakes and join a pilgrim people, what baggage must be left behind? What do I need/want to discard in order to travel light?

Travel light means resiliency, mobility, responsiveness to new movements of the spirit in yourself and in others. *Travel heavy* means slow to respond, limited in movement, fixed horizons, control.

if you would travel light what do you need/want to leave behind?

Try it in the style of a backpacker. The backpacker takes careful inventory of everything laid out to go into the pack. The weight of each object is assessed. Some items are repackaged into lighter containers. Less useful items are set aside as being too heavy for the trip. Think of yourself as backpacking in life. What goes into the pack you carry? What could be repackaged? What do you need/want to leave behind in order to travel with resiliency, responsiveness, and a minimum of heavy pressure?

One *Gifts of Silence* group, after spending time in individual meditation play-acted the children of Israel departing from Egyptian captivity for the wilderness. As they moved out of camp each person placed a symbolic object or a written description on the fire to represent a weight he or she was no longer going to carry. We did not know what each other's weights were; we did realize that everyone needed/wanted to discard something in order to *travel light.*

People in *Gifts of Silence* weeks and weekends have found it helpful to act out the new birth process. Acting it out seems to open the body to send messages that are obscured by much talking. Working in teams of two, the one unfolding into new birth or new beginnings curls up tightly on the floor, making a closed ball with the body. The unfolding member of the team then begins the slow, careful process of opening the folded person. A resistant hand is massaged until fingers begin to uncurl. Clenched fists are patiently opened; arms are gentled into a reach. Carefully, and never roughly or by invasion, the folded person is brought into a sitting position. Trust is encouraged and eyes that were shut open. Ankles and knees are flexed, tense places are soothed, challenged to relax. The person is brought to a standing position, arms stretched, ready for take-off. A friend has led the folded person into readiness for soaring.

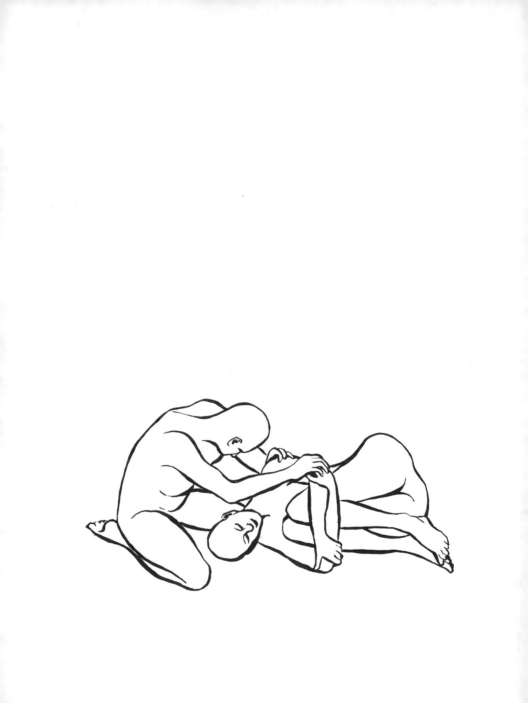

Once a young man in a *Gifts of Silence* weekend said he would like to be born again and experience new birth, new beginnings. The group wanted to help this happen for him so they formed a long birth canal with two rows of people facing each other. The young man began to squirm at one end, working his way through the rows of friends who were pushing him but also offering enough resistance that he had to struggle himself. At the birth end of the canal others were calling him by name, urging him into his new world. He struggled. His friends struggled. He made it! The shouts of all his friends calling his name welcomed him in rebirth.

Birth is never easy. If you have borne a child or have been present at the birth of a baby, you know how much energy is used, how much pushing, urging, persistent labor is involved. Why expect something different from new beginnings, new births, new pilgrimages? Each new birth leaves its mark. When the baby loses the umbilical cord, there is the navel as a badge of gestation and birth. In some Christian traditions when an infant is baptized the child is passed from person to person until everyone present has had the opportunity to mark the child's forehead with the sign of the cross, another badge of birth. To be marked is to be alive and growing. What a wonder to be human with every moment open to new birth, new beginnings, new pilgrimages, new markings.

thanks be to God

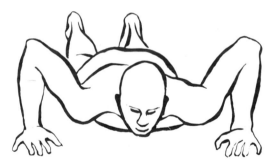

I will be close to the earth

thanks be to God

I will be close to myself

Celebration

Silence,

Refine me.

Wherever a *Gifts of Silence* group has gathered its time together has ended with a Celebration. This is a time of completion and a time of beginning. Bread and wine are at the center, either in eucharist or in simple sharing of common life.

Much preparation goes into this Celebration. Wine is bought. The bread that is baked is sometimes dark, coarse, and chewy, sometimes filled with fresh herbs, and once it was fresh Mexican sopaipillas. Aromatic herbs, juniper wood or pitch are gathered for the incense. Always someone appears with candles, rough sand casted ones delicately balanced on a cholla candelabra or ordinary household candles. Often there is the glow of a fireplace, maybe a campfire. Offerings are prepared—a poem, an *ojo de dios*, a flower, shell, a symbolic object, a painting. These offerings are given to each other while the bread and wine are placed in the center. Usually there is neither traditional chalice nor paten. Once tin cups for everyone to use were provided as an offering. The wine pouring from the jug into those tin cups made a good, simple sound.

Everyone shares in preparation; everyone has a place in the celebration. Each individual celebrates interior space while the group ritualizes for each other opportunities for illumination, ecstasy, thanksgiving, joy. At the moment of offering bread and wine become powerful symbols of life from God that flows into all persons. The treasures of a week or weekend are offered and poured into the flowing stream of history. Someone recounts a story from childhood, another tells the story of God's call to Abraham, another shares hopes for the future, another tells a story from the Gospel, someone reads a lesson from Scripture, another reads a newspaper article. The past, present, and future are offered up together.

The importance of ritual has been brought home to us time and time again as we have participated in these concluding-beginning celebrations. The ritual has never been elaborate. It has been more eclectic than representing one source. There has always been spontaneity in both planning and execution. There has been much repetition in the ritual. Persons' actions have been intense and different from everyday. During the week or weekend participants frequently have experienced critical events in their silence, emptying, story telling, and rebirth. The ritual seems to be a profound way of dealing with these critical events. It occurs to us that ritual is a community action in which the individual can seal the private event into the whole in such a way that alienation is diminished and a common unity is affirmed. Persons who have shared these experiences have asked: "why is it that after so much time spent in individual and group silencing and emptying, we seem more able to worship as a community?"

When we probe for what lies behind this question it is usually some form of paradox that emerges. The idea of silence, meditation, and emptying might be expected to isolate individuals and make it more difficult for them to participate in group celebration. And yet the experience behind the question is just the opposite. Another stereotype behind the question is that meditation is a way of disengaging from other people and from the urgent issues of the world. In the *Gifts of Silence* celebrations people find themselves drawn more closely to their fellow celebrants and also more deeply engaged in the issues that face our time. Not only does a probe of the question lead to paradox, but usually someone comes up with a comment such as: "We have a great deal to celebrate. That's why we are more able to worship together."

At this point there is a temptation for the group to embark upon a *how awful it is* trip and downgrade their usual worship experiences. Someone points out that the reason some worship lacks meaning is that *at home* there hasn't been much life together during the week previous.

When the group gets back on the track of thinking about the here and now of their *Gifts of Silence* experiences these symbolic words are used in the discussion to push the thought processes further:

death
liberation
boundary
unity
simplicity
commitment

How is death a part of the Celebration?

In the emptying process an individual occasionally goes through a profound death experience. In the setting of meditation, care, and guidance, this death experience is positive. It releases a hidden fear of death and creates a powerful inner peace. This inner peace becomes the source of courageous action. If a person has died, is there anything in the world to be afraid of? This is one of the meanings of Christian baptism: when I go down under the water I symbolically die and share in the death of Christ. When I come up out of the water death is left behind and I symbolically share in the new life of Christ. This is sacramental language that describes the *new life* of the person who has passed through death.

Even when a deep experience of one's own death does not happen, the person who silences and empties will still come to grips with death forces, interior and exterior. These may be powers that warp a whole nation; they may be powers that torture the individual. When a person comes face to face with these powers, recognizes them as death producing forces, and names them by name, the person is more able to cope with the interior powers and generally becomes more politically involved in the struggle against those powers that warp the human family.

Out of the death experience comes rebirth. Emptying, dying, silencing is like the seed that falls into the ground, dies, and bears much fruit.

Some of the people in *Gifts* have shared their new understandings of the cross as the result of their own death experiences. On the Cross Jesus died in a state of complete emptyness and powerlessness. His death is the death of the incarnate God who put himself completely into the hands of death forces. Resurrection is the victory over these false powers that are now unmasked in the presence of true life power. These discussions in *Gifts* about the Cross and Jesus' death lead eventually to an analysis of life and death forces in our world today and what it means to walk in the way of Jesus before these death forces. James Douglass reflects: "This valley is empty like the soul of Jesus on the Cross. I begin to understand its liberating power in this emptiness, a way of life in which the silence of a void is the beginning of all understanding and power."

How is liberation a part of the Celebration at the close of a Gifts of Silence *experience?*

During the week there have been break-throughs in persons' faith stories. What was hidden or dreaded is broken open and affirmations of the power of life in their stories are made. These exciting break-throughs are resurrection dimensions in the faith story and can be celebrated through the biblical language of the resurrection of Jesus. When this happens the resurrection is seen in a new light as opening up the future that was closed, or dreaded, or hidden. Imagine a whole human community standing with its back to an open tomb, standing on the edge of that tomb with the future coming as a gift toward them! The tomb is open; the future is open; it comes as a good gift to be trusted. One teenager participant put it this way:

The Lord has created the Heavens and the Earth.
Every creature is endowed with unique beauty.
Every stone, tree, bush has a story all of its own.
Beauty and sound are all around, if we could but perceive.
The moon and the sun light our path.
But we are the ones who must open our eyes.
Rejoice, all of you,
The door of your tomb is open.

Once this open tomb, open future, is perceived, people begin to challenge whatever in life would again close the tomb, either for the individual or community. Interior forces and political powers that would keep the future closed to oppressed peoples are challenged. This direct link between meditation and political action is clear. The bridge is the liberation of open tomb.

But what of boundary? How is boundary celebrated?

The celebration of boundary is not the celebration of limits. It is the celebration of being on the edge or growth line. In silence we discover the boundaries of our existence and in so doing we stretch the growth edge. It is at the boundary that new scenery appears along uncharted pathways. It is more comfortable, for a little while, to stay away from boundary situations, but that leads to boring retracing of too familiar paths. In friendships and in marriage it is the boundary situation that brings life to the relationship. This symbol of boundary as the place of life is used by Paul Tillich in *On the Boundary:* "The boundary is the best place for acquiring knowledge." He also uses the call to Abraham, a symbol used over and over again by *Gifts of Silence* groups: "this God, the God of the prophet and of Jesus, utterly demolishes all religious nationalism—the nationalism of the Jews, which he opposes constantly, and that of the pagans, which is repudiated in the command to Abraham. For the Christian of any confession, the meaning of the command is indisputable. He must ever leave his own country and enter into a land that will be shown to him. He must trust a promise that is purely transcendent. . . . the command to go from one's country is more often a call to break with ruling authorities and prevailing social and political patterns, and to resist them passively or actively."

Then how does unity come into the celebration picture?

The radical polarity between black and white, liberal and conservative, east and west is dissipated in meditation by the vision of the unity toward which the human spirit struggles. The celebration of this unity often includes a prayer in the spirit of Teilhard de Chardin:

Lord Jesus, you are the centre towards which all things are moving: if it be possible, make a place for us all in the company of those elect and holy ones whom your loving care has liberated one by one from the chaos of our present existence and who now are being slowly incorporated into you in the unity of the new earth.

The radical vision of the unity of all things in the center of one God makes most separations trivial. Petty differences fade before this overpowering vision. Tragic separations, war the most tragic of all, are seen as tragic unrealities, untruths, lies. Separations that occur because of ideological, or economic, or social differences are seen as products of distorted vision. The old differences, so important to the success cult, fade away.

And then, simplicity can be celebrated with much joy.

 The celebration of simplicity is an acknowledgment of internal strengths that are endowments from God. Environment can influence the commitment to simplicity, and with this reinforcement from surroundings the emptying process reveals the barren nature of the life that must be surrounded and supported by external forces. Octavio Paz, in *The Other Mexico,* writes of a society impoverished of being while surrounded by many things: "It is a strange ailment, one that condemns us to incessant development and prosperity—by means of which we multiply our contradictions, inflame our sores, exacerbate our tendencies toward destruction. . . . Progress has peopled history with the marvels and monsters of technology but it has depopulated the life of man. It has given us more things but not more being."

Our very nature is reflected in our way of having things, so closely are *being* and *having* related. When competition and acquisition are the power sources for our having, then the having may reflect a being whose security and identity have been sacrificed to the materialistic culture. There is a kind of carelessness about simple having that sets in when a person catches a vision of how frail and of little value *things* are in the life lived in the presence of God. Simple having makes it possible to enjoy and celebrate simple, beautiful, useful things without being possessed by them.

Language is like things. In conversation we can surround, insulate, ourselves with language that decorates our being with many things. Day by day in *Gifts of Silence* groups we have observed the simplification of language toward a more direct, undecorated form of communication that becomes most powerful in the silences at the end of speaking.

Simplicity, unity, boundary, liberation, death, all lead finally to the celebration of commitment.

Gifts of Silence weeks or weekends are times of decisions and commitments that occur in as many dimensions as there are persons in the groups. When the final celebration takes place many bring an awareness of a deepening commitment to trusting, emptying, knowing, new beginnings. But far beyond this the greatest gift of silence is to meet the silent, powerful, loving force that calls us into being. This force speaks in silence. Some have called it God, others the Knower, some call it Power. All who have silenced themselves and moved deeply into silence beyond personal silence know and trust this Presence.

Lord, into your hands I commend my spirit.

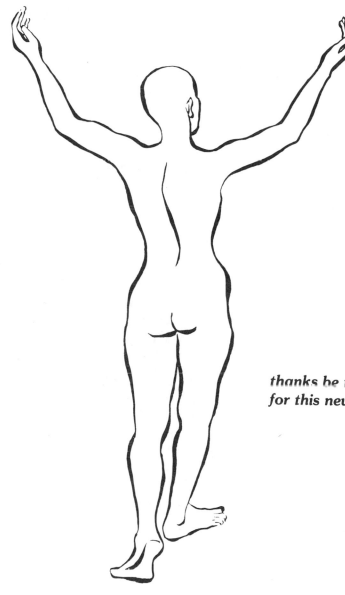

thanks be to God
for this new day

Salute to the new day

*thanks be to God
for this new day*

for all that is around me

for the earth beneath my feet

*for the sky overhead
the sun and the rain*

for all I will experience

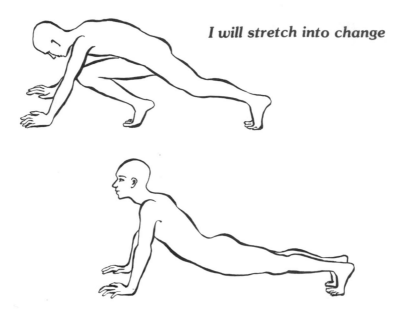

I will stretch into change

I will stretch into new relationships

I will be close to the earth

thanks be to God
for this new day

I will be close to myself